The God

Of

All

Comfort

A study of Comfort and Strength

Pastor Paul M. Caprietta

The God of all Comfort
A Study of Peace and Strength
By Pastor Paul M. Caprietta
Copyright © 2016

ISBN: 13-978-1500647889
ISBN: 10- 1500647888

Copyright number

Published by Caprietta books
Pico Rivera, California
www.divineministriesinc.org

Printed in the United States of America

Disclaimer

The information contained in this book is based upon my experiences and views on the subject that was ministered to me by my heavenly father as the God of all comfort. I am not a medical professional therefore the information is based on my experiences as a pastor for many years and the people I have prayed for, and encouraged thousands of people and therefore I can attest to the experiences to be true and accurate based on the word of God – found in the Holy Bible.

Therefore, if you are willing to get help and find answers to relevant questions. The answers are based on my experiences, knowledge and information taken from the Holy Bible. The Holy Bible will offer all the help and solace you need to overcome any problems that you are presently going through or problems that you may be faced with in the future. Please take time to know the author of the Bible, my heavenly father and your future father as well.

Reasons why this book is important to everyone.

We all go through difficult times in life and therefore we need someone who can offer us hope, mercy, grace and solace in life. In my opinion, the one person who can offer us hope and is willing to provide the comfort necessary for us to walk in victory is Jesus Christ.

I based my conclusion on witnessing and offering hope to so many people over my twenty – three plus years of experience in ministry. This God I am offering to you, my reader, and to people in general has a proven track record for thousands of years. If He helped billions of people the world over He can surely do it for you as well, if you put your trust in Him. The key to your peace and comfort is having a relationship with Jesus Christ – our soon and coming king.

The question I ask you my reader, if you have tried everything else in life to no avail, why not give Jesus Christ a chance. This God, is the God of all comfort providing peace and safety to so many people in the world.

We all have seasons of trials, temptations and difficulty as well as we have seasons of joy, peace, fulfillment and happiness. Life is made of two sides of the spectrum good times and tuff or difficult times. No one is excused from what life brings our way. However, we must be faithful to God. He - meaning Almighty God will bring you through every difficult situation that you may face in your life. I choose to serve the God of all comfort, who will comfort me in every situation that I will ever face in my life.

I can safely say if you put your trust in Jesus Christ he will do the same for you. The Bible teaches that God can keep you in perfect peace whose mind is stayed upon Jesus Christ because you put your ultimate trust in Him. If you do not have a relationship with Jesus Christ, please direct your attention to page 100 of this book and pray the salvation prayer now because time is running out fast and He is a God who has compassion on everyone, and He is the God of all comfort and He wants to comfort you in your time of difficulties.

Foreword

I find this book to be very informative and real for people who are going through difficulty in life. Every oppressed or depressed person should read this book for their peace and strength of mind and refer others as well, who are going through difficult times. My desire is to provide help, and as many people who need the necessary assistance, and steer them into a life of victory, Jesus Christ.

If you do not believe me with the statement mentioned above, just pick up the newspaper or look at the television and you will understand what I just wrote above. Depression is as real as it gets and unfortunately, we play a blind eye to the reality of the causes of depression and the effects it plays on society.

It is reported that billions of dollars are spent on prescription medication for helping people on depression and billions of dollars are spent due to lack of productivity on workers unable to work at their prospective jobs.

My desire as mention in this book is to help as many people as possible with biblical counseling and through prayer. I am confident that people will get the necessary help, if they direct their attention to the God of all comfort, who is found in the Holy Bible the only true and living God available to help you and is willing to help you because He cares deeply for you and about the things you are presently going through. Please do not be pigheaded, "so to speak," and seek the necessary help to walk in victory in Jesus' name.

Love always,
Pastor Paul
Divine Ministries

Preface

I wrote this book as a licensed and ordained minister of the gospel of Jesus Christ for several years, I have had the awesome responsibility of counseling and praying for thousands of people who have gone through many difficult times or are presently going through some difficulties in their lives.

We are living in a very difficult, stressful and challenging times. People need someone who can offer them strength, peace and comfort, who can be found only in the God of all comfort, Jesus Christ the only true and living God found in the Holy Bible. My intention in writing this book is to provide people with strength and comfort and ultimately allow them to walk in victory.

The reality is that, in this world you will have trials, tribulation and stress but take courage I will help steer you into a relationship with the prince of peace, Jesus Christ. He came into the world to offer peace to hurting people.

My desire is to help strength God's wonderful people and help them to walk in complete victory.

"Cast all your anxiety on him because he cares for you."

1 Peter 5:7

The scriptures clearly teach us in the book of 2 Corinthians verse 1:3 "Praise be to the God and father of our Lord Jesus Christ, the father of all compassion and the God of all comfort, who comforts us in all our troubles."

God desire all His children to walk in peace and victory, but unfortunately, we are bombarded with the cares of this world and at times we put our focus on the things of this world and not on Jesus Christ, who is the sustainer and comforter of our souls. Please put your trust in Jesus Christ and you will see a major difference in your life and your life will never be the same.

Remember, reader he is the God of all comfort, and he will comfort you in all your troubles, anguish and pains that is very encouraging news to me and it should be comforting and encouraging news for you as well.

There are too many problems that people are faced with in life and if they do not have the proper channel to let their stress level down, they can suffer with major diseases, which ultimately results in spiritual and physical death. I choose to direct my attention to the only God who cares for us so much that he sent is only begotten son, in the personality of Jesus Christ.

Love always,
Pastor Paul M. Caprietta
Divine Ministries

Table of Contents

Chapter 1

Introduction to Comfort

The Lion in his comfort mode, just relaxing

Chapter 1
Introduction

We live in a society where trials and difficulties are a part of life and if it is not address properly people can live in a state of oppression and depression, ultimately leading to destruction in one's life.

Depression is not a nice condition to live in, and with, and unfortunately some people do not seek the proper help from the appropriate personality starting off with almighty God, godly medical professional or godly Christians to help them during this difficult time in their lives.

The word comfort is a very important quality to God, because the word comfort and any relatable word to comfort, such as the word comfortable, comforter, comforts and comforted appears over one hundred and twenty times in the Bible. In addition to note that the word comfort is used over thirty-one times in the New Testament alone, if providing comfort to people is important to God, it must be important to you and me, in providing comfort to hurting people.

My desire as mentioned in my opening preface I would like to see everyone I meet, live life in peace and contentment. Loss and grief are inevitable in life; however, we can see it through with God's help. We all go through different stages in our lives and thus we should channel our loss and grief in the proper manner, so that, we can get the necessary help, restoration and recovery can be our victory.

Too often we attack people that are closer to us and in the process, we run people away from us. God is calling us into a life of victory and stability.

I am not writing this book in the capacity of a person who has arrived, but on the contrary, I am writing this book as a person who has been touch by what people go through in life especially people who are close and dear to me.

You can take the opportunity to get a copy of my awesome and life changing book entitled, "I am Alive!", available on amazon.com by searching caprietta books.

Later in the book I will give some scenarios of loss in my life and how I handled it, and how with God's help I subsequently walked in victory. I have learned from a very early age in my life to put my trust in my heavenly father whom is the sustainer and rewarded of my soul.

Dear reader, do not be afraid to grieve. Grief is a necessary and vital part of life and if you go through the proper process it can bring strength and a time of refreshing, which ultimately leads to rejoicing.

The Bible teaches,

"Now is your time of grief, but I will see you again and you will rejoice, and no one will take away your joy."

John 16:22

As I recalled if Jesus said you will rejoice again you can count on what he said, because he is the word and he keeps his promises. You will rejoice. God is a God of promises and if he said it, you can believe it, because He is not slack concerning His promises towards us.

Chapter 2

Why Comfort is needed?

Observing a bird having a relaxing stroll
on the beach, and if the birds can do it
we can as well

Chapter 2
Why Comfort is needed?

A very important concept to understand is we all go through difficult in life as mentioned previously. However, if we do not go through times of comfort and rejoicing we will live in depression. Depression is a state of being depress and a period of self-worthlessness and feeling of no value to yourself and to others.

Too often some people play the self-righteous game and they do not allow other people to go through a time of grief. When an individual can go through a successful period of grieving only then a time of comforting can take place in the life of a person.

I always instruct people to grieve on your own time so to speak, but I also inform them that the period of grief should not be too long so that the grieving process become a time of depression and dismay in the life of a person.

There are so many studies out there stating what a successful grieving period is or should look like. The best answer to this question is to allow people to go through the grieving process in a timely manner yet offering them peace, comfort and safety during the storms.

Some people say a good time frame to have a successful grieving period is about two years after their trauma. As mentioned earlier in this book I am not a medical professional, but on the contrary, I have been counseling and praying for people for over twenty-three years. I can truly say I am in a good capacity to offer people a time of encouragement, peace and a time of refreshing by steering them in the presence of the Lord. I can safely say that I have a good track record, because of having a relationship with Jesus Christ in that, I have seen so many people received the necessary help they needed and some of these same people are now living in victory with God's wonderful help, and helping other people that are going through difficult times.

I encourage them to read their Bible, pray and allow them to read some spirit-filled books which will offer them peace and comfort. I steer them to Jesus Christ our risen savior. I will now illustrate a real-life example that took place in my life personally.

My brother, Keith pass away in May 2004, which was a tremendous shock to the entire family. He was supposing in good health, because he had just completed his annual physical and everything seems to be good. My family was going through a very difficult and stressful time on the death of my brother, whom I loved very much. Therefore, thank God, he used me in an awesome way to provide strengthen to my family with prayer, encouraging words and just being there to support them. In other words, I was the strength and safety net for my entire family especially my mother. After his burial, my mom will go to the grave site every month.

After returning from the grave site my mom will go into a state of euphoria and will cry for days. Her blood pressure will sky rocket on seeing the grave site of my deceased brother.

She did that for about 6 months, until I told my mom she should stop going to the grave site because if going to the grave site you are getting so sick, it does not make any sense at all. I said to her, mom do you think Keith will be happy with you getting so sick after seeing his body?

She said, to me "No" and she got the picture I was trying to paint in her mind. Therefore, she subsequently stops going to the grave site on a regular basis and her health condition became better. The High blood pressure she was suffering from is being regulated and I am trusting God for her complete healing.

The Bible teaches,

"Dear friend, I pray that you may enjoy good health and that all may go well with you, even as your soul is getting along well."

3 John 2

I further informed her Keith is not there that is only the shell of this body. My mom understood what I was telling her.

My reader, this may sound a bit harsh but I had to protect the health and well-being of my mother whom I love dearly, we must understand once someone die in Christ, it is not a doom and gloom situation that we think.

Therefore, the family and friends must see the person who died in Christ as a celebration of the person's life and not a dismal feeling of death and gloom.

Remember, God do not take a Christian life on the contrary, God receives the person unto himself. Whenever, I participate in a home going celebration (funeral) I share this statement with the deceased love ones, it literally lifts the countenance of everyone that hears this life-changing statement were lifted and comforted in the Lord.

We serve a wise and loving God who can do exceeding and beyond what we can even think or imagine, because of his great love for every one of us. The God we serve desire that none perish but all come into repentance.

The Bible teaches,

"I will turn their mourning into gladness; I will give them comfort and joy instead of sorrow."

Jeremiah 31:13

"We are confident, I say, and would prefer to be away from the body and at home with the Lord."

2 Corinthians 5:8

Chapter 3

Strength in providing comfort

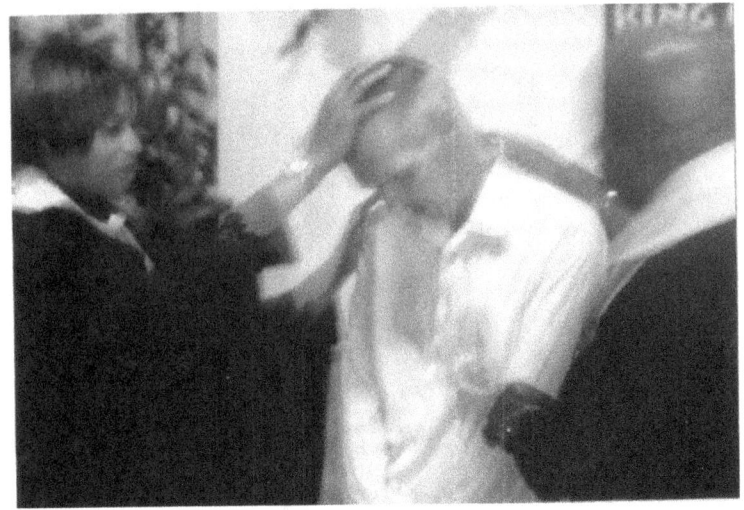

Ministering comforting words in prayer to a brother in need

Chapter 3
Strength in providing comfort

There is tremendous strength that can be accomplished if we channel our grief in the right way. Therefore, if we look at grief as a personal testing and a period of growth in our lives. No one likes trials, but as I said before it is necessary to bring us into maturity. If may be a difficult time we are going through and yes it may feel so at times.

However, if we look at our present situation and we think we are the only ones going through difficult times. My reader, stop for a moment and know that there are people all over the world that are going through, difficult times as well, but take solace and comfort that everyone go through times of testing and difficult.

The Bible teaches,

"A righteous man may have many troubles, but the Lord delivers him from them all."

Psalms 34:19

My reader, let us dissect this scripture the Bible teaches the righteous may have many troubles. Let us look at the word righteous. Righteousness speaks of right standing with God.

It does not mean that you have never sin, but on the contrary, when you do sin you have an advocate with your heavenly father in the personality of Jesus Christ, our risen savior.

You can go to your heavenly father and repent for the sin or sins committed. Once you repent honestly from the heart you will be made right with God and your relationship is restored and not broken.

The Bible teaches,

"If we confess our sins, he is faithful and just and will forgive us our sins and purify us from all unrighteousness."

1 John 1:9

The important concept to grasp is going through difficult is just a part of life and see your difficult as a stepping stone for your advancement in life.

Do not look at the trials you are going through as something you have done. Sometimes it can be something you have done wrong and sometimes it is just part of life.

My reader, take solace from your problems as a time of growth in your life. If we do not go through any difficulty in life, life will be boring and there will be no obstacles for us to conquer in life and subsequently no victories to show we serve an awesome God who cannot fail.

The Bible teaches,

"I was young and now I am old, yet I have never seen the righteous forsaken or their children begging bread."

Psalm 37:25

As mentioned the word of God called you righteous, if God called you righteous. God is during your difficult and He (God) will bring you through it, if you have the right attitude in the God in whom you serve. Please stay committed and serve God with a pure heart, knowing that God "has your back" so to speak.

Too often I see people miss out on their blessings by having a very distasteful attitude towards their heavenly father and blame God for the problems they are presently facing in life.

We must learn to stop that type of mindset and see problems coming into your life because life brings its problems and difficulties. Sometimes problems come because of poor choices we make in life. Please take comfort that God will not allow you to go through more than you can handle, but through it, He will make a way of escape.

The Bible teaches,

"In this world, you will have trouble, but take heart I have overcome the world."

John 16:33b

Chapter 4

Areas people need comforting

Enjoy God's creation helps to provide
comforting times to the weary soul

Chapter 4
Areas people need comforting

There are several areas in life that people need some form of comforting. In my opinion, comforting can come from any area that the recipient needs some form of comforting in life. Loss comes in several different ways and format and thus comfort can come in many forms as well.

We must learn not to take a clavier attitude to people's loss. We must learn to comfort people during their times of loss, because the reality of life is that, everyone will experience some form of loss in their life.

In my many years of ministry I have notice people requiring comfort in so many areas. I am a person who do not judge or minimized people areas of comfort but on the contrary, I listen and provide the necessary comfort to help strengthen them during their times of need.

Sometimes too often people minimize other people's anguish and thus we do not provide them with the proper tools necessary to help them walk in victory.

If we live long enough we will experience some type of loss in life and will need some comforting as well to bring us through, from a life of despair to a life of victory.

I will now endeavor to list some areas I believe that comforting can be applied. The ones listed below are not limited to the only areas that comforting can administered.

- Loss of loved ones or a loved one which can include family members and pets.
- Loss of a job.
- Divorce of a spouse.
- Divorce of a parent, from the children.
- Sporting games.
- Loss of material wealth.
- Loss of material possession such as through fire and natural disaster.
- Students failing their examination.
- Loss due to poor health.
- Misplaced items that are important to us.
- People mistreating you, which include ungodly words being meted out to you.
- Physical abuse
- Mental abuse
- Sexual abuse
- Retirement from a job or the changing of a job

- Changes in life
- Loss of weight, due to sickness
- Unable to finish a project at work or school.
- Students unable to secure proper grades in school.
- Lack or no self-esteem.
- Loss and or feeling abandon.

There are so many areas that people need comfort in, and sadly people come up with areas all the time they need comfort. There are much more areas in which we will further assist people in the areas of comfort. Providing comfort is a quality that is needed more and more in these last and closing days. The enemy of our soul is rearing his ugly head and he will not stop until he has people tormented and walking in defeat. There are so many acts of evil meted out to others in mass shooting at schools, cinemas, shopping malls, the workplace and even recently the co-pilot of an airplane crashing the into plane in the French Alps. There are so many more time will not permit me to document all these ordeals.

With these sorts of catastrophe taking place in the world, that brings about so much hurt and despair in the hearts and minds of people. Hence the reason why so many people are living in stress and need someone to offer them some form of comfort. The church of the living God should and always be a place where people should run to for comfort in these difficult times we are presently living in, because as mentioned earlier in this book that life is made up of turmoil and we need someone who can offer us hope and comfort.

Chapter 5

The things people fine comfort in

Pastor Paul delivering a comforting message to people who needs an encouraging word

Chapter 5
The things people find comfort in

When I look around in our society I find some very disheartening ways people find comfort in. I will list some of the things where people find comfort and solace in, to help them in their times of comfort. They perform some very grievous ways to destroy themselves and others.

1. Over eating
2. Eating disorders
3. Alcohol
4. Illegal drugs
5. Prescription drugs
6. Sexual activities
7. Injuring themselves and other people
8. Acting out violently
9. Isolating themselves from love ones
10. Feeling of guilt and despair
11. Operating in fear
12. Operating in paranoia
13. Depression
14. Anxiety
15. Excessive sleeping

16. Insomnia
17. Excessive shopping
18. Obsessive behaviors
19. Abusive activities
20. Additional activities people find Solace in, can be a wide variety of Ways.

I like to encourage people when they are going through difficult times, they need to turn to Jesus Christ who can offer them hope and they can find strength in Him in times of need.

I am not making light of anyone situation, but on the contrary, I am also willing to help people. I serve a God who cares for everyone on the earth.

The Bible teaches,

"God is not willing that any should perish but that all should come to repentance."

2 Peter 3:9

I further encourage them to keep their eyes on Jesus Christ and that God will not give them more than they can handle, but through their difficult times He (meaning) God will make a way of escape for them.

I have been through many difficult times in my life, and I tap into God's strength to help me and thank God, He truly cares for each one of us. I recall the account of David in 1 Samuel 30:6 The Bible teaches that "David was greatly distressed because the men were talking of stoning him; each one was bitter in spirit because of his sons and daughters. But David found strength in the Lord his God.

Chapter 6

Benefits in providing comfort

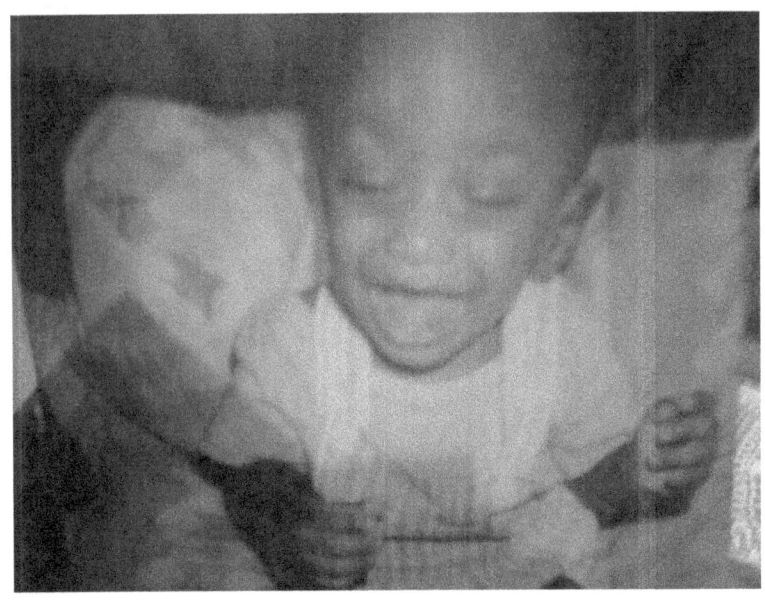

A child enjoying a happy moment –
laughter is good as medicine

Chapter 6
Benefits in providing comfort

There are tremendous health benefits to be derived from providing comfort to the needs of the recipient and for the person who is administering the comfort and the encouragement.

First to the person who is providing the comfort and the encouragement, you offer hope to people that are going through some difficult times and that gives you a sense of belonging and providing help to someone else.

Secondly, you realized that you are doing your God given assistance to humanity. Third, the scripture states it is better to give than to receive and there is joy and contentment when you service others knowing that whatever good deed you do for someone it will come back to you if not to you personally but to your family members.

The benefit for the person who is receiving the comfort and the encouraging words. First, it relieves stress which could prevent high-pretension, heart disease, and all types of major diseases.

The person receives a sense of happiness and enjoyment in their lives. Laughter is like medicine to the soul. Please take time to enjoy the happy times in your life. God has invested tremendously in your life. Therefore, take time to enjoy life and live your life to the fullest potential.

Secondly, the medical profession showed individuals who lived in a state of high anxiety and stressful lifestyles were about five times more likely to suffer heart disease than non-stressful individuals.

Therefore, it is extremely important that we take care of the temple God has entrusted to us by eating a diet low in sodium and unhealthy fats and exercise on a regular basis to maintain a healthy weight. The United States of America has too many sick and disease individuals which brings untold financial burden on the country and on the individual who is sick. We need to take care of our health, so that we can live life to the fullest potential in Jesus Christ.

I encourage people to take time to read your Bible or a good book so that they can take time off their busy schedule and have a time of peace. We need that time of relaxation in our lives so that we can be comforted. If we serve the God of all comfort, please seek Him for all your comforting needs.

The Bible teaches

"Be still, and know that I am God; I will be exalted amount the nations, I will be exalted in the earth."

Psalm 46:10

Chapter 7

Comforting scenario 1

Pastor Paul sharing another comforting word to the graduation class of 2013

Chapter 7
Comforting scenario 1

This account started off very difficult for me in December 2004. My earthly father was going through a sickness in the year of 2004 and he was believing God that I will come and visit him at his residence in Brooklyn, New York. We will communicate regularly over the telephone and things was going very well indeed. Over the thanksgiving weekend I told him I was coming to visit him when the kids get off from school on vacation around the second week of December 2004.

On December 3^{rd,} 2004 around 6:00pm I received a telephone call from my mother and sister that my Dad whom I loved very dearly had just pass away which was very devastating for me because I was coming to see him and was unable to see him alive. I felt very disappointed no seeing him alive, I was rest assured by the scriptures that I will see him again in Heaven because he died in Christ.

My father gave his life to Jesus Christ on September 1995 in our wedding ceremony. Therefore, knowing that he had passed was bitter/sweet for me.

The reason for my decision of bitter/sweet moment. The bitter moment was he was having some difficult with pains in his body and if the Lord did not heal his body it would be better for him to be with his savior in Heaven.

The sweet moment was he died knowing Jesus Christ as his personal savior and that gave me much joy. My reader, it is very difficult for your love ones to die without knowing Jesus Christ as their savior.

So, I went and visit my mother and siblings at their Brooklyn, New York residence and had some very encouraging and comforting words to administer to them, which was received with great anticipation and joy.

Therefore, while offering some encouraging words to my love ones over the Christmas holidays a very disturbing new was aired on the television on December 26th, 2004 with the tsunami on the continent of Asia. While I was providing comforting words to my family in Brooklyn, New York. The people needed some strength and comfort on the continent of Asia with the dreaded news that over 250,000 people lost their lives with that terrible disaster. Some families lost most of their family members, while other lost some members.

My family drew strength from the fact only that only one person passed away in our family and yet whole families probably passed away from the disaster in Asia in 2004.

Sometimes we are going through difficult times and we feel that it is only us going through these difficulties in life and yet if we look around we would realize how many people are facing difficulties in their life at the same time. We can draw strength and encouragement from each other when we are having a difficult time.

The Bible teaches,

"No temptation has seized you except what is common to man. And God is faithful, he will not let you be tempted beyond what you can bear. But when you are tempted, he will also provide a way out so that you can stand up under it."

1 Corinthians 10:13

As a young child, I believe God blessed me with the spirit of comfort and encouragement and I found myself encouraging people during my young years until I progress to adulthood. This gift of comfort and encouragement manifested in a greater depth as a teacher.

I found myself comforting and encouraging so many students during my vocation and the gift of comfort and encouragement was in more evident when I became a born-again Christian and now a Pastor.

I recalled when I attended church on one day, a visiting Pastor from one of the Caribbean island called me out and gave me a prophetic word.

The prophecy was given to me on 02/10/95 is listed below: -

"God has placed a compassionate heart upon you to help people in destitute and desperate situation. He sees me praying, admonishing and counseling people."

-   Pastor G. Garraway

I thank God for giving me the gift for helping and encouraging people and some of these people called me when they are going through difficult times. I offer and pray with them and direct them to read their Bible and meditate on the word of God which brings strength to them and fulfillment to me.

As Pastors and leaders our mandate is to provide them with strength and stability. We do not have all the answers to their problems. However, we can steer them to the God all comfort in the personality of Jesus Christ, who has all the answers and not just have all the answers, he is willing to meet them at their point of need and help them through their difficult times.

My responsibility is to steer people to God and ask the Holy Spirit – who is the third person in the godhead (ELOHIM), the spirit of truth to minister to them and lead them into a greater relationship with God.

*"**But thanks, be to God He gives us the victory through our Lord Jesus Christ.**"*

1 Corinthians 15:57

Chapter 8

Comforting words Scenario 2

A beautiful flower is pleasant to your heart and adds comfort to your soul

Chapter 8
Comforting words
Scenario 2

This scenario is very troubling to me because one of our friends a young lady who we helped had some major problems. She lied on us and general she did not spoke the truth. She makes up stories on a consistent basis to get our attention. For example, she will claim she is sick at school because she felt threaten in school and will cry out for help by making up untold stories.

One of the stories she made up was she was sick in school and throw up due to an upset stomach. The school called me informing me that she is sick. Therefore, I went to the school to pick her up and on my way, I felt in my heart she was not speaking the truth concerning her illness.

When I picked her up and we arrive at home I told her to go and lie down on the bed to get some rest. She turns to me and said, "Paul I am not sick and I am not tired."

Therefore, I turn to her and asked her why she would make up that story and said you was sick. She turns to me and said, "I was just making up the story because I did not want to be in school today so I made up the story to come home quickly."

She further said that she was being bullied by a young boy, which we found out that it was not true. In my opinion, that was a loss to her because she was always speaking untruth and need constant words of comfort and affirmation to remind her that when you do not speak the truth you hurt other people which eventually spiral down into hurting more people and cause a lot of turmoil and make things very difficult for others.

Her area of difficult was not speaking the truth and in my opinion, that was a serious loss – the loss of not speaking the truth, which some people overlook as not being serious. The Bible teaches that God desire truth in the inner man.

We are responsible for speaking the truth to people so that people can trust us. It is very important to speak the truth because it can blow up and make things worse. As mentioned above a loss of lying and furthermore lying on others is even more detrimental because it brings unwanted discomfort and turmoil in the lives of others.
The question I asked my reader is, why people do these distasteful things to others to bring unwanted harm to other people.

Chapter 9

Comforting words Scenario 3

Pastor Paul delivering an inspiring and comforting message

Chapter 9
Comforting words
Scenario 3

I recalled I met a young lady who was going through a very difficult time with the loss of her dog. She considers the dog to be part of her family for over ten years.

This scenario is very touching to me because it did not involve a human being but an animal, a pet. Some people will have minimized this because it pertains to a pet. Being from another country we do not put so much emphasis on animals as being part of the family as compare to a human being.

Therefore, it was unique for me to console and comfort someone on losing a pet. Therefore, I had to call upon the Holy Spirit for wisdom and guidance on how to properly administer godly counselling to meet the needs of the young lady. Remember, reader a loss is a loss and it does not matter what type of loss you incurred, it will affect you greatly if the thing loss was dear to you.

I minister the word of God to her and she felt much better on hearing God will perfect everything that concerns her and He will strengthen you. I further informed her that God will not give you more than what you can handle but He will make a way of escape for you. I told her to take time to grieve and allow a proper grieving process for you to go through. She further asked me "How long should I take in my grieving process." I told her that you take your time in the grieving process and you will know when it is time for you to move on and get the victory.

During the writing of this book I saw the young lady and she said to me "thank you for helping me during my time of difficult." She further said, "That you will be surprise Pastor to know that I found a dog that look like the dog that I lost." She further said, "The dog was the same color and look like my previous dog (pet) that I lost." I said to her praise God and she hugged me and was very excited about her replacement dog. We just must trust God to bring everything to pass if we put our trust in Him. Thank you, Jesus, for helping this young lady.

Chapter 10

Comforting words Scenario 4

Pastors Paul and Gail relaxing enjoying each other's company

Chapter 10
Comforting words
Scenario 4

In this scenario, it was the most touching of all and yet very life changing and disheartening all at the same time. As a Pastor, I look for ways to minister to the needs of people that are hurting. I will attend a local convalescence home to visit the elderly and pray for them.

I will look for ways to minister to the needs of these elderly people by visiting them and find how they are doing. They will be so happy to see me or a matter of fact anyone who will just spend some time with them. I attended the home from time to time due to my very busy schedule therefore the management of the home became known of my title. When visiting these elderly people, I will spend between forty-five minutes to one hour. I will pray with them, read a few Bible scriptures with them and just encourage them. I am surprised about the wealth of knowledge some of these seniors possessed because I am a lover of history and general knowledge.

Some of the seniors were very forgetful and anytime I go and visit them they will ask me "who are you?" I will give them my name and they repeatedly ask me my name. Some of them will ask me "when am I coming back to visit them." They will have asked the question while I am still chatting with them.

On one occasion, there was an elderly lady by the name of Gail. She was living at the convalescence home for eight years and she knew most of the occupants in the home and was very knowledgeable about history and general knowledge which was a blessing to me just to listen to her wealth of knowledge. She mentions that there are so many people living in this home that do not have anyone visiting them. When I inquire, I found out that there are occupants that do not have any visitors for six months or more.

In my opinion, this is one of the greatest loss that anyone can experience in life. The loss of feeling and being abandon by their love ones. I feel this is a travesty to abandon your parents who did so much for you in your early stage of life and because they become older or are elderly you just drop them off at a convalescence home and leave them there to die.

These elderly people literally grieve because they do not see their love ones and the only people they see are there medical professionals.

May we rise as a people of compassion and go and visit these seniors. They do not matter who you are if you are a human being and grace them with your presence. Just take a little time out of your busy schedule and go and visit them. At times, I will take my children to see these seniors and it is a trill just to see their faces. Their countenance is lifted on seeing these lovely and adorable children. Unfortunately, I have not visited these homes for a while due to so many other ministries activities the Lord has directed me to conduct.

Chapter 11

My personal views on health Benefits

Enjoying God's creation, which relieves
stress and provide comfort

Chapter 11
Views on health benefits

I strongly believe that there are tremendous and additional benefits to be derived from working towards having a comforting life or walking in victory in comfort.

These are some of the additional areas I believe will be helpful.

- Participate in some form of physical activity daily. This can be achieved by walking, doing household chores which will allow you to sweat. Far too often we believe that we must go to a gym. Therefore, because of this mindset we believe we cannot engaged in some physical activities.

- Another benefit is getting the adequate amount of sleep, so that you can rejuvenate your body through resting your body. Some studies recommend seven hours a night whereas other studies report eight to ten hours of sleep.

- In my opinion, I believe you should get the required amount of sleep that is beneficial for you, so that you can perform at your optimum level.

- Having some form of spiritual connection. For example, going to church services regularly, going to prayer meeting, meditation classes and or any area where you can find peace and solace.

- Eating the right types of foods and beverages can help prevent mood swings in the life of an individual. We need to cut down on fatty, sugary and food high in sodium.

- Having a support group for men only or women only. Some people prefer having a combination of both men and women in the group. I have decided to have my own support or fellowship group, with this group I founded is called, "Divinely Inspired Men." With this group men, can share their shortcomings, with other men who will not judge each other. Whereby, people can laugh and pray with, and for each other.

These are some of my recommendation for walking in comfort, which ultimately allow you to walk in victory.

- Set a time of the day as your down time or I love to say do nothing time. In other words, a meditation time, where you can reflect on the goodness of God in your life, or even taking a stroll in the park or walking on the beach.

- Watch some clean and hilarious comedy, so that you can relieved some stress in your life, through laughter. The Asian culture, do some form of tai-chi

- Read some uplifting and inspirational books like the Holy Bible and other religious books, for example you can go on Amazon.com and search Caprietta books.

- Have some spirit-filled friends that can provide strength and words of encouragement.

- Listen to gospel and other inspirational music such as praise and worship music, clean instrumental music and any music that relaxes the soul.

- Attending seminars that will help strengthen you. Please remember, to research these seminars to see whether it is wholesome and not destructive in nature.

- Playing some form of sports, that get your interest, so that fun can be achieved and help release or eliminate the stress in your life.

- Be part of a brotherhood or sisterhood group, whereby we can be transparent. Remember, transparency is the key to achieving your deliverance. My wife is part of female birthday club, where her girlfriends meet once a month and share gifts, food and have a lot of fun with each other. Another, is having a Bible class, where they can share the scriptures and they learn from each other.

Chapter 12

Words of comfort

Painting is comforting to the soul

Chapter 12
Words of comfort

During the writing of this insightful and encouraging book I found myself on the receiving end of being comforted by some friends of mine during a situation I and my family were going though. We were lied upon by someone in whom we were very dear too. She said some very disturbing things about me and my family which she attempted to put a wedge between us.

Therefore, because I provided comfort to so many people for so many years it was very fitting and encouraging to know we found very refreshing words of peace from some associates and people who turn out to be very good friends in time of need.

We serve such an awesome God who cares about everything that we go through. I thank God for these people that He placed in our lives during the trials and tribulation that we were going through as a family. God will always send people to encourage you and the devil will always send people to discourage you with the attempt to destroy and assassinate your character.

The Bible teaches,

"Therefore, there is now no condemnation for those who are in Christ Jesus."

Romans 8:1

I will now take the time to illustrate to you the different ways Satan uses people to further destroy you with ungodly words.

Let us look at the account of Job he was a blameless and upright, a man who fears God and shun evil. However, job went through some serious testing in that, Job lost his children, animals and was stricken with sickness and diseases and yet Job did not sin by charging God with wrongdoing. "His wife said to him, "are you still holding on to your integrity? Curse God and die!"

What is extremely important to me was his reply, "He said you are talking like a foolish woman. Shall we accept good from God, and not trouble?" Additionally, if we go further to read about the account of his three friends in the book of Job 2:11-13. Reader, we should be extremely careful in whom we take counseling from, because not every counseling is of God and therefore we should look unto God for peace and sustenance.

My God is just wonderful and He loves and cares for everyone and everything we go through. We are walking in victory by and through the power and blood of Jesus Christ. I want to encourage each one of you my reader, we all go through difficulty as mentioned several times in this book. However, we need the God of all comfort, whom comforts and display his compassion towards us.

The Bible teaches,

"Therefore, there is now no condemnation for those who are in Christ Jesus."

Romans 8:1

Satan is always looking for ways to destroy us, but thank God for his mercy and grace towards us and He is willing to comfort and strengthen us. Thank God, we were vindicated and the truth was revealed and we claim the victory in Jesus wonderful name.

Chapter 13

The pyramid of comfort

Chapter 13
The Pyramid of comfort

In most aspects of life there is a basic pyramid structure. Now, I will endeavor to illustrate the stages, as based on the medical profession people go through and if not address it can leave to destruction of an individual life or many people lives. Far too often people do not seek comfort from the right channel and therefore there is a tremendous breakdown in our society.

In my opinion before we walk in victory in comfort, we may go through these stages of resentment and fear, but if we allow ourselves to go through these processes we will get the help we are seeking. These stages can help lead us into a successful process of comfort.

The medical profession reported that there are some stages that people go through in life when they are faced with trauma in their lives. I have decided to take my own direction towards explaining these basic stages that most people go through, including myself as a Pastor.

When faced with a traumatic situation a person can either faced it head on and get the necessary treatment or they can have delayed the treatment which can result in further defeat in one's life. It all depends on the individual with regards to the support system they are willing to go through.

The Stages I have decided to illustrate on are not limited to the ones mention below-

- Denial – In this stage I will call it the "owning stage." In this process, the quicker an individual decide to own up to their problems or short-coming, it is easier for them to get the necessary help, which can lead them to walking in victory.

- In my opinion, this stage is the most difficult stage, because no one likes to admit their short-coming, but on the contrary, in this stage it will either make or break you. Therefore, admit it and get help as quickly as possible.

- Anger – In this stage an individual starts to draw back into phases or euphoria, thereby feeling a sense of guilt, which may lead to violent behavior to one's self or others.

In this phase, the person who is comforting the individual needs to be there to walk him or her through their difficult time, so that they can get the necessary help as soon as possible. I love to pray with and for these types of people on a regular basis.

- Bargaining – In this stage people starts to say what I could have done to prevent me from going through this stage. Life throws us some difficult situations and we just must go through these times in life having good friends and a great support system, knowing that we all go through difficulties in life and it is all part of life.

- Acceptance - With proper help during these stages as mentioned above. We can accept the fact that when difficult times comes our way, we just should realize that people go through problems in life and we must ask God for strength during these times.

- I will encourage people to know you are not in this situation by yourself and with caring people around you, and having a support system you will make it through in victory. Remember, the same comfort you offer to others, the same comfort will come to you.

Qualification to be Born-Again

Ephesians 2:8-9

For by grace you have been saved through faith, and not through anything that you have done. It is a gift from God, and did not come about through working for it, in case anyone wants to boast.

1. Admit that you are a sinner, having broken and transgressed against God's laws, and need a savior. Romans 6:23

2. Believe in Jesus Christ as the son of God, who died to pay for our sins. John 3:3 and John 3:16

3. Repent for your sins. Romans 10:9 and 1 John 1:9

4. Accept Jesus Christ as your personal savior and Lord. John 3:3

Please direct your attention to the next section, and pray the salvation prayer. The Lord is waiting for you, my reader, to come to Him because of His awesome love for you. His arms are wide open to accept you into the body of Christ. He paid the ultimate price for your sins.

He is waiting for your response to Him, so you may have life more abundantly. Life is too precious to waste and He will give you a life to your fullest potential in him.

To the unbeliever and the person who wants to give, or re-dedicate their life to Christ, please pray the Salvation prayer on the following page.

If you made a commitment to live for Jesus Christ for the rest of your life, please e-mail me and let me know of your new birth experience. See my contacts page.

The Salvation Prayer

Dear Jesus,

I come to you just as I am, a sinner and I confess all my past and present sins before you. Help me to live a truly Christian life in accordance with your word. From now on, dear God, I will live only for you, by your grace and mercy. Thank you for saving me, in Jesus' name.

If you have prayed this prayer and believe in Christ in your heart, the Bible states that you are now born-again.

"I tell you the truth: no one can see the kingdom of God unless he is born-again."

John 3:3

Celebrate your new birth by finding a home-church where the undefiled and pure word of God is taught. The Lord will equip, strengthen and encourage you to live a life that is above reproach.

I would like to know that you are being taught well, advancing in the things of God, making valuable contributions to the kingdom, and most importantly, that you are putting to flight demons who are oppressing people.

The Lord will work through you, if you allow Him to do so in the process, therefore don't hesitate to send me an email and let me know how you are doing. See my contacts page.

We hope that you enjoyed this valuable time of teaching with Pastors Paul and Gail Caprietta.

If you would like to contact Pastors Paul and Gail Caprietta for additional copies of this, or his other books, schedule a speaking engagement or check their events, please contact:

Pastors Paul and Gail Caprietta

Co-laborers in Christ

www.divineministriesinc.org

Office: 562-806-0969

Email: **Pastorcaprietta@hotmail.com**

Scripture nuggets on Comfort and strength

"The lowly he sets on high, and those who mourn are lifted to safety."

Job 5:11

"Wait for the Lord; be strong and take heart and wait for the Lord."

Psalms 27:14

"So, do not fear, for I am with you; do not be dismayed, for I am your God. I will strengthen you and help you; I will uphold you with my righteous right hand."

Isaiah 41:10

"I have told you these things, so that in me you may have peace. In this world, you will have trouble. But take heart! I have overcome the world."

John 16:33

"The salvation of the righteous comes from the Lord; he is their stronghold in time of trouble."

Psalm 37:39

"Cast your cares on the Lord and he will sustain you; he will never let the righteous fall."

Psalm 55:22

"The Lord is a refuge for the oppressed, a stronghold in times of trouble."

Psalm 9:9

"God is our refuge and strength, an ever-present help in trouble."

Psalm 46:1

"The Lord is good, a refuge in times of trouble. He cares for those who trust in him."

Nahum 1:7

Who We Are in Christ – Part 1
By Pastor Paul M. Caprietta
Order code: WWAIC1

This book is a divine inspiration for people all faiths. It teaches us to glean and practice knowledge, wisdom and insight. From the author's poignant message and stories. I absorbed profound values to live by in today's world.

> Bonnie Priever
> Former rabbinical studies student
> Los Angeles, CA

You did a great job of putting many pertinent and inspiring biblical references into a short but impacting book. It helps me to understand and build my relationship with Christ at a very critical time in my life. Thank you for putting this book together.

> Marina White
> Former Student
> University of California

Who We Are in Christ – Part 2
By Pastor Paul M. Caprietta
Order Code: WWAIC2

Who we are in Christ is what the world is missing. A personal relationship with Jesus Christ. This book is an inspiration for all new believers and for those who desire a refresher course. Who We Are in Christ is also about the questions being asked and answered.

Rev. Dr. Melvora E. Moore- Fulton
Step-Out on Faith Ministries
Los Angeles, CA

"In my 57 years of preaching and teaching God's word I can truthfully say that Pastor Paul Caprietta's message of Who We Are in Christ is timely and life-changing for a time such as now. Every excited believer should read this book!"

Rev. Dr. Edward B. Skeete
International Global Fellowship
Los Angeles, CA

Life as Immigrants
By Pastors Paul M. and Gail P. Caprietta
Order code: LIFE

As an immigrant, myself, I find this book to be accurate of the struggles we go through during our migration process. Everyone should read this book so they may understand the life of an immigrant.

> Luis Espinoza
> Graphic Designer
> Downey, CA

While the book illustrates the struggles of one man to make a new life, it resonates the struggles that all immigrants face regardless of ethnicity, nationality, politics, creed and religious background and class. Ultimately, it emphasizes the role of community and the need for community to first serve and then prosper.

> J. Gutierrez
> School Teacher,
> Los Angeles, CA

I Am Alive – The Account of a Transformed life
By Pastor Paul M. Caprietta
Order Code: ALIVE

I thank my loving, and adorable husband Pastor Paul for this life-changing book. God, bless you Pastor Paul for putting this awesome book together.

Pastor Gail Caprietta
Divine Ministries
Pico Rivera, CA

Pastor Paul did an awesome job in documenting his life journey for all those who are interested in being blessed. I will recommend this book to everyone who is not living life to their fullest potential in Christ Jesus.

Michael
Ardent Reader
Los Angeles, CA

Crisis in the Church – Parts 1 and 2
By Pastor Paul M. Caprietta
Order Code: CRISIS 1 & Crisis 2

In these two books, Pastor Paul M. Caprietta is a necessary read for our mindsets to undergo change, because {the world is} in need of salvation; by how can they be [saved] when the church, as we know it, is in such crisis.

> Dr. Melvora E. Moore-Fulton
> Step – Out on Faith Ministries
> Los Angeles, CA

I am always lifted and inspired by the books authored by my brother in Christ, Pastor Paul M. Caprietta. He is truly chosen by God and I refer to these writings on a regular basis to reassure my own sermons.

> Dr. Joseph Johnson
> In His Hands Ministries
> Los Angeles, CA

Parenting and Nurturing Foster Children

By Pastors Paul M. and Gail P. Caprietta
Order Code: PARENT

Being adopted as a child, it takes courage to face the unknown, not just for the child but also the caregiver and I feel Pastors Paul and Gail have helped those children a great deal. I am truly blessed to can read this book. It's a reminder that even if you don't have all the answers. God will be there to help, if you only take the time to ask.

> Nikki Walsh
> Former Foster/Adopted Child

This book communicates the power of God in a family's life when they purpose to serve precious children. The children's letters and pastor's Paul own personal testimony relayed in this book, are a testament to the blessings of God.

> Patricia West
> Pediatric and Adult Occupational Therapist

Know you Adversary
By Pastor Paul M. Caprietta
Order Code: ADVER

I find this book to be a great book. It is life-changing and very much a book that everyone can relate to and everyone should get a copy of this awesome book. People are under attack by the schemes and techniques of the enemy of their soul.

> Michael
> Ardent Reader
> Los Angeles, CA

Get your Own Sheep
By Pastor Paul M. Caprietta
Order Code: SHEEP

This book is about leaders dealing in unscrupulous activities. Some of these said leaders and Pastors stealing other leader's sheep. The church of the living God need to step up to the plate, "so to speak" and do the right thing. Leaders need to stop playing Church and do the right thing, which is winning the lost to Jesus Christ. This book is about evangelism and discipleship.

The Art of Marriage
By Pastors Paul and Gail Caprietta
Order code: MARRIAGE

In this awesome book, you will learn the purpose for marriage and both the challenges and blessings of being part of the greatest union on earth. I will expose you to practical solutions to problems people face in marriage.

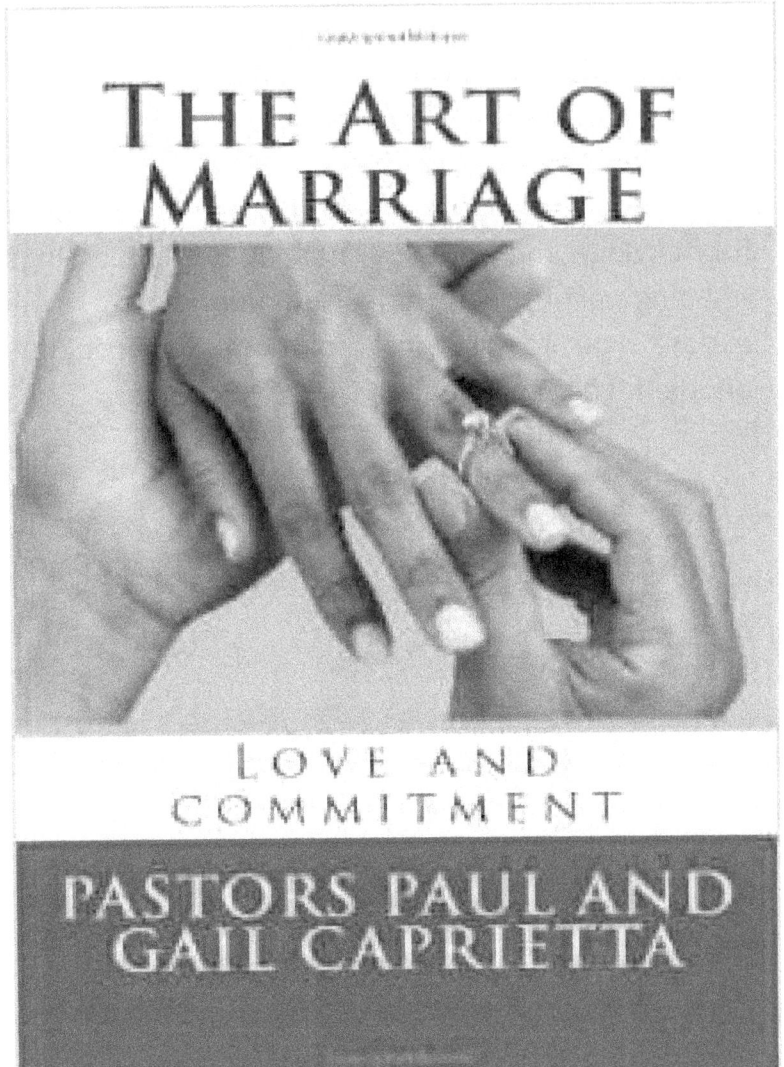

Acknowledgement

I want to thank my heavenly father for giving me the material to write this life changing book for people that are going through difficulty in life to gather some strength and to help other people to be strengthen. Additionally, we must understand that people need some encouraging words because society has so many problems and they need some form of outlet from their problems. God desire for all his children to walk in victory and live life to the fullest potential in Him. God desire that we walk in perfect peace.

Conclusion

As a Pastor, I am touched when I look around and see so many people living life in depression and under the control of the enemy of our soul. We must work towards helping people that are going through so much turmoil in their lives.

The Suicide rate in the world has reach an alarming rate and sadly we depend on the wrong people to offer us hope. Sadly, to say the people who claim that they can offer hope are unable to provide people with the right kind of care and we allow people to live in fear and depression. I once hear an individual said, "Allow people to grief in their own time." I asked them what that time is. Some of them will say, "If it takes years let them be."

I am not a medical professional, however, how can you allow a person to grief for 5 years and over on an ordeal they went through? We should use wisdom and common sense in whatever we do in life.

Additionally, some people are seeing a therapist for over ten years. We need to realize if something is not working please seek assistance from another qualify professional. May God, give you His strength to overcome all your ordeal in life.

Look for exciting new titles by visiting

Caprietta books on Amazon.com and be a blessing to the kingdom of God. Please refer all family members and friends

In 2016 -2017

Go to: www. Divineministriesinc.org

The Lovely Pastors, with a special thank you.

When I look around in the world today, I see so many people living with so many problems and my heart is full of compassion to help these people. The research shows that there are so many different types of depression. I will take the opportunity to list a few: -

- Anxiety disorders
- Eating disorders
- Bipolar disorders
- Depression
- Dissociative identity disorder
- Nightmare
- Obsessive compulsive personality disorder (OCPD)
- Schizophrenia

These are some of the types of diseases that leads to mental health, and I believe some of these disorders or depression started off with a loss in the life of an individual. Some of these losses were not dealt properly with, which subsequently leads to some of these types of depression.

In my opinion, these are some of the reasons why I believe that proper help must be addressed early in the grieving process for getting help, proper comfort is vitally important for a successful life.

The research shows that there are over 450 different definitions of mental disorders. In my opinion that is extremely alarming and yet, some medical professional does not want to accept the fact that they need some form of spiritual assistance to make their clients or patients better.

The almighty God order of creation is spirit, soul and body, but unfortunately so many medical professionals only address the soul and they neglect the spirit realm. I believe if they address the spiritual being first, by addressing the patient spiritual need, and subsequently progress to the soul. In my opinion, I have seen most of the times that if I address the person spiritual needs first and further work on their soulish needs later and I find everything sometimes works quicker.

Some of these medical professionals only like to medicate these patients and eventually you see what happens to some of these people.

Some of these patients are so addicted to pain medication, they rely on it so much that some of them over dose on these very medications which was intended to help them.

Some of them commit mass murders for example, schools, malls, airplanes, just to name a few of the gross acts of evil that is taking place in the world today.

Additionally, the medical profession when dealing with people with mental health diseases should take a lot of time, effort and prayer to see these patients live up to an optimum level in life. Too often they take a clavier attitude towards mental health, and some of these doctors become a catalyst for pushing their medication. It is reported that 57.7 million people suffer with some form of mental health disease and on average one in five Americans suffer with mental illness each year.

We need to take this area of mental health very seriously and do not brush it off as a minor problem. We need to wake up and ask God to help us and direct us on how to go about addressing this destructive disease.

I am willing to do my part and pray and ask God for direction for the medical professional to work through this major problem affecting so many people in the world.

Let us all do our part to help these people, the clergy should be praying regularly, the medical professional should be doing a better job at diagnosing these patients and providing the necessary help for overall wellness.

In addition, the pharmaceutical companies should be working at getting a better product on the market.

Finally, the FDA should be working at all the side effects before approving a drug. Therefore, we all have a major role to play in our society so that optimum health is for all people, all the time. We must stop playing games with people lives and work towards getting people the necessary help. We should stop playing the blame game, where each institution blaming each other, instead of working together to bring about change for ever one.

I want to thank you very much for helping me market this life-changing, awesome and uplifting book for people of all faith to be inspired and encouraged by, because people are going through very difficult times in life.

Please refer this book to as many family members and friends as possible so that people will be delivered from stress and problems in their life. I am encouraging all my readers to refer this book to all your family members and friends.

I know this book will help them by working on the areas set out in this book. I want to set them free from the techniques and schemes of the enemy of our soul – the devil.   Victory is only possible by having a relationship with Jesus Christ, my savior and Lord.

Comforting Photographs

"Do not be afraid of them; the Lord your God himself will fight for you"

Deuteronomy 3:22

"For you have been my hope, sovereign Lord, my confidence since my youth"

Psalm 71:5

"May your unfailing love be my comfort, according to your promise to your servant"

Psalm 119:76

May the blessings of Almighty God be upon you today.

Love you, very much and may you walk in all God's comfort.

Note Taking

Note Taking

Note Taking

www.ingramcontent.com/pod-product-compliance
Lightning Source LLC
Chambersburg PA
CBHW070114290526
45789CB00005B/2025